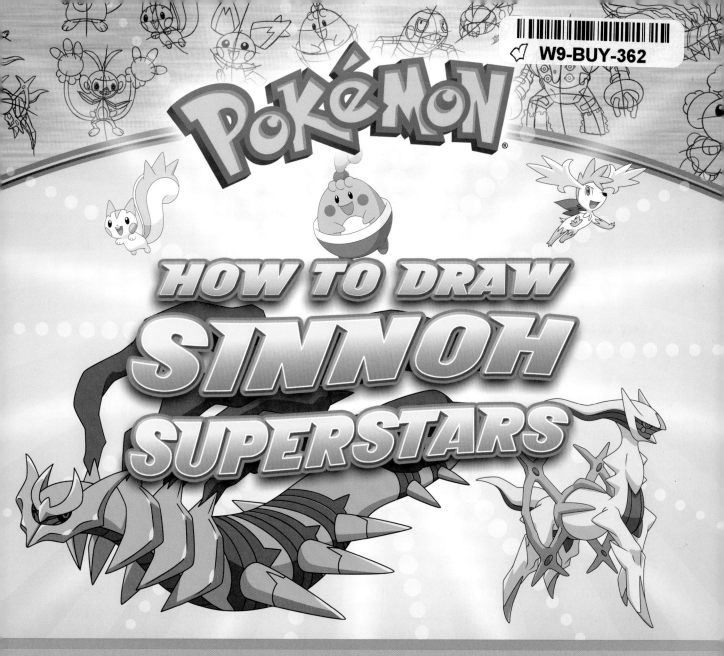

POKÉMON

HOW TO DRAW SINNOH SUPERSTARS

WRITTEN AND ILLUSTRATED BY RON ZALME

ISBN: 978-0-545-22625-7

12 11 10 9 8 7 6 5 4 3 2 1   10 11 12 13 14 15/0

Designed by Cheung Tai
Printed in the U.S.A.   40
First printing, January 2010

SCHOLASTIC INC.

New York	**Toronto**	**London**	**Auckland**
Sydney	**Mexico City**	**New Delhi**	**Hong Kong**

More to Draw than Ever Before!

Are you ready, trainer? In these pages you'll find a whole host of new Pokémon to explore and draw. Arceus, Giratina, Shaymin, and many more await your pencil.

Before you begin your quest to capture these elusive Pokémon on paper, you're going to need the proper gear. Here's a few ideas to get you started.

The Basic Tools

- **Pencil** — Any basic graphite pencil can accomplish most drawing needs.
- **Paper** — Photocopy paper or tracing paper is terrific for sketching.
- **Eraser** — Try a soft one that won't smudge and has "edges" to get into tight spots.
- **Rulers, circle guides, ellipse (oval) guides, and shaped curves** — These help create a smooth, finished look for your drawing.
- **Color** — Try pens, markers, colored pencils, watercolors, paints, etc.

Your Training

In the pages that follow, fourteen of the most elusive Pokémon have been reduced to a series of simple steps. All good drawings start with just a few sketch lines, a framework upon which to build a drawing, so the first steps begin with several action lines (drawn in soft black pencil) and a few basic shapes (in blue) to define the Pokémon's pose. From there, each step adds construction shapes and detail.

Once the sketch is done, your task will be to refine it! Use your eraser to clean up foundation lines, then darken the linework you're happiest with. The last step shows the character without the sketch lines so you can evaluate how your drawing should look when finished.

After that, it's up to you to decide the next step. Add color, textures, shading . . . and whatever details make your Pokémon look impressive!

The Basic Shapes

When you draw with pencil and paper, you're actually working with flat two-dimensional shapes, circles, ovals, squares, rectangles, and triangles.

However, an artist must think in terms of three-dimensional shapes. This helps to create an illusion of depth and volume that makes your drawing look more exciting and realistic! The 3-D shapes you'll use are: spheres, cones, cubes, cylinders, and pyramids.

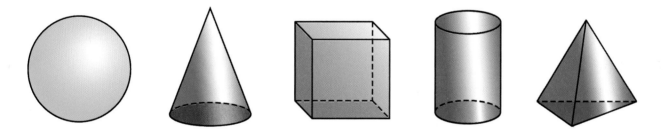

Ready, Get Set . . . Go!

Okay, trainer, those are the basics. Drawing takes practice, so don't get discouraged if you don't get the results you expect right away. Keep at it, and your confidence in your abilities will grow.

SPIKY-EARED *PICHU*

Pichu, known as the Tiny Mouse Pokémon, is the pre-evolved form of Pikachu. These tiny Pokémon store electricity in their cheeks, but they're not very skilled at it. When they're amused or startled, they often give off random discharges of powerful static electricity!

First, draw the two arching action lines (shown in black). Using their placement as a guide, sketch the large circle for Pichu's head. The two crisscross guidelines on the head will give it a 3-D appearance and help you align the features. Next, draw the body shape and feet.

Now that the head is in place, you can sketch in the two large ears! Use the crisscross guides to locate the eyes and mouth. Then move on to the arms.

③ Most of the major construction is done, so you can start adding detail now. Pupils, cheeks, thumbs . . . and a tail too! Add the "M" shapes to define the interior detail of each ear.

DRAWING TIP:
Carefully judge your sizes and proportions as you sketch. A misplaced line early on can strongly affect the way your drawing turns out.

POKÉMON FACT
Pichu "play" with each other by touching tails to shoot off sparks! This game is also a test of courage.

④ Darken the eyes, add a tongue, and you're almost done! As you finish, smooth out the angular construction lines to give a more natural feel to your character.

⑤ Clean-up time! Grab your eraser and carefully remove the sketched construction lines you used to build your drawing. Save only the linework that defines the character, then enhance those lines with darker pencil or pen.

BUNEARY

Buneary are able to deliver powerful blows by uncoiling their ears. These hits are strong enough to injure an adult human! Buneary also have impressive jumping abilities.

2
Use the guides to locate and sketch the eyes and mouth. Then add the ears and arms in the positions indicated. Note the short, straight vertical line that defines the attachment of the head to the body.

1
Start with just two action lines, then pencil in the three large ellipses (ovals) that will become the head, body, and foot. Note how the crisscross guides on the head oval strongly indicate the direction Buneary is facing. Use a half-oval shape to define the foot in the rear.

3 Think fluffy! Using smooth circular shapes, add fluffiness to Buneary's body and ears. Next, add some detail to the features — the pupils and nose.

DRAWING TIP:
Always sketch lightly! Build the drawing slowly and darken your lines as you become certain you have drawn them correctly. This way, the unwanted lines will be much easier to erase.

POKÉMON FACT

It is believed Buneary can only be found in Eterna Forest, located in the Sinnoh region.

4 Can you see Buneary come to life? Just a little more detail is needed. Darken the eyes, add a tongue, draw the finger lines, and sketch in the tail!

5 Compare your drawing to the original example. Did you get it right? Make adjustments if you need to, and then clean up with your eraser and go to finish!

HAPPINY

Happiny always wants to carry a round white stone in its pouch in imitation of Chansey, the Pokémon it will eventually evolve into.

1 After sketching in the action lines, the real trick to drawing Happiny is the large oval shape that defines the entire structure of its body. So work carefully until you're sure you've got it right!

POKÉMON FACT

Despite its cuddly appearance, Happiny has amazing strength and can carry many heavy items . . . even other Pokémon!

2 Widen your original oval at the bottom to allow for the pouch area and move on to sketch the features and hair. Note how the small floating oval in the last step is altered here to become a curlicue . . . every object has an underlying basic shape to structure it around.

3

Sketch in the arms and legs, then go ahead and add some more detail to the hair. Use those guidelines!

DRAWING TIP:

If you don't have a circle-guide template, use buttons, coins, cups, and cans . . . anything round can work as a makeshift guide.

4

Darken the eyes, add some trim around the pouch area, and don't forget to add a round object for Happiny to hold!

5

Pink and white are about the only colors you need to finish Happiny, but you can have fun shading the round surfaces of its shape. Look around and observe how the light creates shadow on round objects. Apply your observations to Happiny!

BUIZEL

Buizel is a Water-type Pokémon with an inflatable collar that it can use to float on water effortlessly. It deflates its collar when diving and uses its spinning forked tail as a propeller.

1

Start with the usual arrangement of action lines. Draw the head circle on the vertical line. Next, draw the cross-hair guide for the feature placement. Sketch in four loops as shown, two for the arms and two for the feet.

2

Adjust the shape of the head. Use the circle as your basis and extend a muzzle, neck, and crest off the back of the head. Next come the eyes and nose. Now do the body shape, using your action lines as a map to place it correctly. Basic circles form the water wings on Buizel's arms.

③

Use your face cross-hair guideline and sketch the line that separates the cheeks and muzzle from the rest of the head. From there, you should be able to place the eye, mouth, and cheek designs. Now draw the flotation collar — a big oval around the neck — and finish with the belly line and tail.

DRAWING TIP:

You can shade in your drawing more quickly by holding your pencil on its side instead of using the point.

POKÉMON FACT

Buizel can be playful, but don't let that fool you! This Pokémon is tough and competitive in battle.

④

All the tough parts are done! Just add the tiny details . . . teeth, tongue, toes, etc. Blacken the eye, nose, and cheek design. Almost finished!

⑤

Clean up your drawing and you're ready to finish your character! Why not try a coloring method you haven't used before: crayons, colored pencil, pastels . . . artists are known for their creativity. Go for it!

SPIRITOMB

Spiritomb was formed when over one hundred malevolent spirits were locked away in an Odd Keystone. This was punishment for all the evil deeds the spirits performed when they lived five hundred years ago!

1

Begin with just two simple action lines in the shape of a basic plus sign (+). Draw the eyes along the center crisscross of the lines, and then add a pentagon (a five-sided shape) along the axis as shown.

2

Using each straight side as a guide, add a jagged outside outline, much like a circular saw blade. Make sure the points all face the same way. Sketch six large circles inside Spiritomb's shape.

3 Add a mouth with a crooked shape, then a spiral shape for the eye. Now draw in five smaller circles. Don't forget the large oval at the base of the figure.

DRAWING TIP: A kneaded eraser is a type that draftsmen use. It can be shaped to fit into those tight spaces!

POKÉMON FACT

Spiritomb is one of only two Pokémon with a type-pairing that under normal circumstances has no weaknesses. The other is Sableye, a Pokémon from the Hoenn region.

4 It's time to add four very small circles. Notice that the hard outlines have been converted to softer, smoother "ghostly" lines!

5 Clean up your drawing and have some fun! Remember, all your outlines don't have to be black — consider tracing over the outlines with rich colors. Try colors that compliment each other and colors that contrast . . . experiment!

13

AMBIPOM

Ambipom is the evolved form of Aipom. It has two tails that perform the duties of its hands and arms . . . and with greater efficiency. When Ambipom forms a circle with its tails, it's a sign of friendship!

③ Now that you have the simple framework in place, you can start to refine your drawing with detail. Add the fingers and frills to the tails . . . two hairs to the head . . . and feet. But no hands — Ambipom doesn't need 'em anymore!

① Start your drawing with the usual action lines. Note the bend to indicate the pose of the arms. Next, pencil in the three large ovals: one for the head and two for the hands of Ambipom's tail. Sketch in the body shape and add two sweeping lines for the tails.

② Add the two ears. Notice that one is in front of the head oval and one is behind. This will help give the finished drawing a 3-D effect. Ambipom should be facing slightly to the right and not looking straight at you. Add arms, legs, and tails around the forms you made in the last step, then draw the basic features along the guidelines.

4

You should have all the features in place by now. Darken the eyes and add design detail to the fingers, face, and body. Remember to keep you linework light until you are sure it's placed where you want it!

DRAWING TIP:

Need to trace, but don't have tracing paper? Any nearby window can be a light source to help you see through regular photocopy paper.

POKÉMON FACT

Since evolving, Ambipom rarely uses its arms . . . it uses its two tails to shell and eat nuts.

5

Back to the clean-up step! Erase your unwanted sketch lines and reinforce the lines you keep. Have some fun with this character and try another sketch. You can move the tails around, change the pose . . . try something different!

PACHIRISU

Pachirisu can charge electricity in its cheek pouches and discharge bolts of static from its tail. It protects its stored food with dangerous furballs that are statically charged!

1

After the usual action lines, make a very large oval for the head and add the crisscross guides to it. Next, sketch the ovals for the feet. Where you place them along the vertical action line will determine how long the body will be, so be careful!

POKÉMON FACT

Pachirisu contain so much electricity that if they lose control, they could actually electrocute another Pokémon!

2

Locate and pencil in the eyes and mouth, then the ears. Overlap two small ovals for the front paws. Next, finish the body sides. The tail is just a single squiggle at this point.

3

Continue working on the tail . . . be sure to give it volume! It should be wide enough to touch or almost touch the side of Pachirisu's head. Complete this step by adding the facial features and toes.

5

Go ahead and clean up as usual. Have fun!

4

Final details are all that's needed now . . . three spikes to the tail tip . . . darkening of the eyes . . . teeth. Did you get those electrified cheeks in the last step?

CROAGUNK

Croagunk uses the poison pouches in its cheeks to communicate with others. Its signature move is to catch its opponents off guard with a toxic Poison Jab, a move that can stun both Pokémon and people!

1 Draw the single vertical action line and the two horizontal ones. Place a large circle for the head just off-center of the top axis. Then add an oval for the thigh on the lower horizontal action line. Now you have enough shapes in position to link the body shape. Sketch it in!

2 The features will be easier to place if you draw the oval for the cheek first and then sketch the mouth as a wavy line from the cheek to the other side of the circle. Note that the top and side of the head circle should be altered here to become the proper shape of Croagunk's head. Along the top horizontal action line, sketch the cylindrical shapes for the upper and lower arms, then add the feet.

DRAWING TIP:

Avoid smudging your own drawing by working from top to bottom and from the side opposite the hand you are working with. For instance, if you're right-handed, start at the left.

③ Now that your foundation is in place, sketch in the details: eyes, teeth, mouth, fingers, and toes. You can also start to add the body and arm stripes.

④ Add in the last details . . . pupils, tooth lines, nostrils, and stripes.

POKÉMON FACT

Croagunk evolve into Toxicroak . . . and while both are weak against Flying, Ground, and Psychic-type moves, they are very strong against Grass, Fighting, Poison, Dark, Bug, and Rock-type moves!

⑤ Finish your drawing in the usual way with careful erasing and bolder line work. Ready for a challenge? Now that you're comfortable with this step-by-step method, try doing it with your other hand!

GLISCOR

Gliscor is also known as the FangScorpion Pokémon, Gliscor is extremely rare. It has a more sinister look than Gligar, the Pokémon from which it evolves.

3

Using the ears as your reference point, sketch the eyes into place. After you've added the details for the claws, feet, and tail, begin the construction of the wings. Make sure they stay "behind" the body.

1

Reproduce the action lines exactly as shown and begin roughing in the ovals for the head, hips, and claws. It's important to get the crosshairs for the features just right!

2

Using the crosshairs, place the two large ears atop the head oval and add a mouth line. Next, do the ovals for the feet, then the legs. Add detail to the claws and sketch in a rough circle for the tail barb.

4 The rest is just detail drawn over the foundation you've made! Add teeth, eyes, and body designs. Finish by connecting the tail barb to the body with four same-size circles, one behind the other.

DRAWING TIP:

Blacken the back of your sketch with the side of a soft pencil. Then layer the sketch over a fresh piece of paper and trace the outlines of your drawing. Voilà! You've got a copy of your drawing on the paper underneath!

POKÉMON FACT

Gligar can only evolve into Gliscor when it holds a Razor Fang.

5 After erasing your sketch lines and completing Gliscor, try adding a background. Gliscor is nocturnal and swoops down from trees — you could make a really dramatic scene with a full moon!

YANMEGA

Yanmega is the largest of the known Bug-type Pokémon. Using its wings, it generates ultrasonic waves that can cause major damage to its foes' internal organs!

1 Draw the action lines: vertical for the body, top horizontal for the wings, and bottom horizontal curve for the legs. Continue by placing the head oval at the bottom, with each shape for the body and tail placed behind it.

 Sketch in the ovals on the head, then add the legs over the action lines. Do one set of wings and construct the tail so it resembles an airplane's.

3

Create three spikes along the center line of the back, and then add two more legs. Draw a second set of wings alongside the first. Finish by adding the stripes around the tail section.

DRAWING TIP:

If you think your drawing looks just right — straight, even, and balanced — try looking at it in a mirror. Many artists use mirrors to make sure their drawings look balanced from every angle.

POKÉMON FACT

Yanmega and its pre-evolved form, Yanma, are the only known Pokémon whose names begin with Y.

4

Carefully copy the design on the sides of the head to your sketch, then add all the circle designs to the sides, tail sections, and wing tips!

5

Did you notice we added the fangs? The spikes to the legs? Good for you! Observation is key to becoming an artist. Finish your drawing in your favorite style!

SHAYMIN SKY FORME

Originally known as the Gratitude Pokémon, Shaymin is able to transform into its Sky Forme, which has large, wing-like ears. In its new forme, Shaymin has the power to clean the environment.

POKÉMON FACT

When Shaymin transforms from Land Forme into Sky Forme, its type changes, too. Shaymin Land Forme is a Grass-type, but Shaymin Sky Forme is a Grass-and-Flying-type.

2 Use the long sweeping action line at the top to sketch in long ovals for the ears. Follow the action guidelines to place the body shapes, starting below the head and down to the feet. Next, add the basic facial features along the crisscross axis.

1 Shaymin has very large ears, so make sure you allow plenty of room on your paper for the sketch. Reproduce the action lines as shown and draw a large circle for the head, including the crisscross guides. Then place two smaller ovals for Shaymin's paws.

4

Details, details! Sketch in the pattern on the arms and legs, then complete the facial features. Darken the nose and finish the eye.

DRAWING TIP:

Tracing isn't cheating! It can help you learn size, placement, and proportion until you get the hang of it yourself.

3

Flesh out the structure of the ears by adding to the long ovals you drew in the last step. Draw more loops of hair onto the forehead. Don't forget the tail!

5

Eraser time! Clean up your drawing . . . and don't be afraid to judge it. Omit the lines you don't like and emphasize the ones you do. Finish your drawing with bold outlines, and then color it in.

GIRATINA ORIGIN FORME

Known as the Renegade Pokémon, Giratina is Legendary in the Sinnoh Region. Giratina is the only known Pokémon who can travel between the dimensions of the Reverse World and the normal world.

1 Start with an action line that flows horizontally across your page. Then add three equally spaced vertical lines about a third of the way from the end. Draw an oval for the head and a thick "worm" shape for the body. Add the three lines above the body as guides for the tendrils.

2 Use the tendril guides as a rough template to sketch around . . . you can be creative here and not worry too much about following the example closely. Use the three vertical action lines as a basis for drawing the three legs that wrap around the body just behind the head. Next, add the spikes along the body's sides and tail.

⑤ You're getting there! Use your eraser and carefully rid the drawing of all its construction lines. Now darken the lines you're going to keep and add some color. It's much easier when you take things step-by-step, isn't it?

④ It's time to observe and draw the details . . . the design on the spikes and the bands that encircle the body. Finish the features with more facial detail as well . . . like Giratina's eyes within its armored skull.

POKÉMON FACT

Giratina's signature move is Shadow Force. It can vanish and suddenly attack with powerful energy!

③ Define the shape of the head with the scalloped line. Then add in the three legs on the far side of the body. Put more tendrils on top of the body, then sketch spikes on the ones you've already drawn.

DRAWING TIP:

Animators like to sketch in blue pencil . . . like the way these steps are done.

REGIGIGAS

Another of the Legendary Pokémon, Regigigas is known as the Colossal Pokémon. Legends state that Regigigas once towed continents with ropes! Its powers have not been used for so long that in battle, Regigigas is known as a "slow-starter." But watch out, it improves quickly!

1 Start with the long vertical action line and two horizontal lines that will define placement of Regigigas's shoulders and hips. Then draw a very large circle for its barrel-shaped chest and extend that down a bit for the waist. Add more action lines to frame the arms and legs.

2 Draw the head, which should look like a big tongue draped over the back, and add two ovals for the massive shoulders. Use cylinders to define the shapes for the arms and legs, and two more ovals for the hands.

3 On each hand, draw in three claws grouped within another oval. Then add decorations to the body. The three circles on the chest, to the right of the action line, are just slightly larger than the three on the left. This leaves the impression of being closer to the viewer.

DRAWING TIP:

Artists often use a light source that is above and to the right of their subject for shading. How do you think Regigigas would look if it were lit from the side or underneath? Experiment!

POKÉMON FACT

Regigigas lives in hidden ruins, where it sits as still as a statue. If the land is in danger, Regigigas may awaken to protect the land.

4 Add more details to your sketch: tiny ovals on the head, additional circles on the chest, and rough leaves on the shoulders and as feet. Don't worry about following every little curve as long as the general feel and shape are there.

5 Clean up with your eraser, and then highlight the shapes and details. Compare your drawing to the example. Did you miss anything? Make any corrections necessary and go to color!

ARCEUS

Arceus is the newest Legendary Pokémon to be discovered in Sinnoh. It is said to have emerged from an egg in a place where there was nothing. Not much else is known about this mysterious Pokémon, but there's no doubting its power.

1 Begin with three action lines. See how they begin to form a spine and legs? Along these first sketch lines, place the circle and oval that will form the head and body. Note the guideline in the oval that will help you locate the features.

2 Follow the example and rough in the cylindrical shapes for the legs along the action guidelines. We've broken each into three sections to help make the form easier to identify. Connect the oval to the circle with a neck shape, then complete the construction of the head.

5

Almost done! Use your eraser to remove the unwanted construction sketch lines and embolden the linework that best depicts Arceus! Finish your drawing as you like . . . pen, marker, watercolor, acrylic paint.

DRAWING TIP:

Put dates on your sketches and save them in a folder. Any time you start to have doubts about your abilities, go back and look where you started. You've improved! Keep practicing!

4

All your basic shapes are now in place! Add in the detail to further define the character: facial features, spikes, and muscle lines. When you convert the construction shapes into rougher angular outlines, you'll give Arceus a more rugged appearance.

POKÉMON FACT

Arceus may be the only Pokemon who can change its type. When it does, its color changes, too.

3

Too many shapes at one time can be difficult to handle, so to draw the spikes around Arceus's middle, start with just two. See how they are shaped around the circle you drew in Step 1? Now you can sketch in the other two legs and a tail. Next, add some detail to the face and neck.

You made it!

Congratulations, Trainer . . . you've become an expert Pokémon artist! Keep practicing and you can apply all the tips and tricks you've learned to any Pokémon you wish to draw! All of your favorite Pokémon are just a pencil sketch away.
That's 493 Pokémon in all!